**DO NOT REMOVE
CARDS FROM POCKET**

POISON FANGS

ANIMAL WEAPONS

Lynn M. Stone

The Rourke Press, Inc.
Vero Beach, Florida 32964

PHOTO CREDITS
Breck Kent: p. 13; all other photos © Lynn M. Stone

Library of Congress Cataloging-in-Publication Data

Stone, Lynn M.
    Poison fangs / Lynn M. Stone.
        p. cm. — (Animal Weapons)
    Includes index
    Summary: Describes weapons used by snakes, especially the venomous species.
    ISBN 1-57103-164-2
    1. Teeth—Juvenile literature. 2. Poisonous snakes—Juvenile literature. [1. Teeth. 2. Poisonous snakes. 3. Animal weapons.] I. Title II. Series. Stone, Lynn M. Animal weapons.
QL858.S76 1996
591.57—dc20   96–8998
                                                   CIP
                                                    AC

Printed in the USA

TABLE OF CONTENTS

POISON FANGS

An animal's weapons help it defend itself. If it's a meat eater, the animal also uses its weapons to kill other animals.

Most animals and their weapons are not **lethal** (LEE thul), or deadly, to humans. Certain snakes, however, can be just as lethal to humans as they are to the animals they eat.

Perhaps no other animal is more feared than a **venomous** (VEN uh mus) snake. Venomous snakes make a lethal poison called **venom** (VEN um).

The copperhead, one of the four types of venomous snakes found in the United States, is a pit viper

VENOMOUS SNAKES

Most of the world's snakes are not venomous. In North America, only four types of snakes have venom. They are the rattlesnakes, copperheads, coral snakes, and water moccasins, or cottonmouths.

Australia is the only continent with more **species** (SPEE sheez), or kinds, of venomous snakes than non venomous.

A few venomous snakes live in the seas off parts of Asia and Australia. The others live in many kinds of land **habitats** (HAB eh TATS), or homes.

The colorful coral snakes have fixed front fangs rather than the extra-long, fold-back fangs of pit vipers

VENOM

Snake venom is a cloudy, yellowish liquid. Snakes store venom in glands in their upper jaws. Venomous snakes bite to force venom into their **prey** (PRAY).

Each type of venomous snake makes its own type of venom. Some venoms are more lethal, drop for drop, than others. Certain venoms are more deadly to certain animals than others, too. Bird-eating snakes, for example, produce venom that is especially deadly to birds.

A drop of venom drips from the tip of an eastern diamondback rattlesnake fang

SNAKE BITES

A venomous snake's bite works like the needle that a doctor uses. A doctor's needle is hollow with a tiny hole at the tip. Pressure at the top of the needle forces medicine through the needle and into flesh.

Most venomous snakes also have needles—two hollow fangs with holes at the tips. As the snake bites, it instantly sends venom through its fangs and into its prey.

A Gaboon viper of West Africa swallows a rodent that its long fangs and venom have killed

The tree python's green skin is a perfect match for the Australian rain forest where it lives

Down the hatch! A timber rattlesnake swallows a mouse

VENOM AT WORK

Snake venom contains substances that destroy blood vessels, nerves, and flesh, among other things.

People bitten by venomous snakes should find a doctor immediately.

The bites of North America's venomous snakes rarely kill anyone. The bites, however, can be deadly if not treated properly.

Large snakes usually inject more venom than small snakes. In North America, big rattlesnakes are especially dangerous.

In a tight coil, a water moccasin prepares to strike. The white lining of this American pit viper's mouth earned it the name "cottonmouth"

PIT VIPERS

Pit vipers are a special group of venomous snakes. Like other snakes, they can't hear and they don't see well. However, they have special organs that sense heat given off by warm-blooded animals—mammals and birds. The heat-sensing organs are in hollows, or pits, in the snakes' heads.

Heat sensors allow a pit viper to find prey. A pit viper can also follow the heat trail of an animal its bite has injured.

North America's rattlesnakes, copperheads, and water moccasins are pit vipers.

A rattlesnake's tongue is harmless. It helps this pit viper sense who or what might be in its neighborhood

FANGS

Different species of venomous snakes have fangs of different lengths. Probably the largest fangs are the two-and-one-half-inch long fangs of the Gaboon viper.

Fangs are hard, but they're also delicate. They often break. Snakes have the ability to replace their fangs several times each year.

Rattlesnakes and other snakes with long fangs keep their fangs folded back in their mouths— except when they bite.

These vipers don't show off their weapons unless they plan to use them.

The fangs of this king cobra are not especially long. Unlike the fangs of rattlesnakes, cobra fangs are fixed in place

KILLING WITH COILS

Certain non venomous snakes use their teeth and also their muscles as weapons. These **constrictor** (kun STRIK tur) snakes use their teeth to grab prey. At the same time, the snakes loop their bodies around the animal and squeeze. The loops of the snake are called coils.

The coils squeeze so tightly that the prey cannot breathe. It dies from lack of air, not from crushed bones.

The best-known constrictors are the boas. Most boas are six to nine feet long.

The red rat snake's teeth grip the mouse, and the snake's coils prevent the prey from breathing

CONSTRICTORS

The largest of the boas is the 25-foot long anaconda of South America. Two small boas, neither more than three feet long, live in the western United States.

Pythons are also constrictors. The largest is the reticulate. It's about the same size as an anaconda. A big reticulate python weighs over 200 pounds.

North America's rat snakes are constrictors, too. These include the colorful red rat snake and yellow rat snake.

Glossary

constrictor (kun STRIK tur) — a type of snake that kills an animal by coiling around it and squeezing its body to stop breathing

habitat (HAB eh TAT) — the special kind of place where an animal lives, such as desert

lethal (LEE thul) — very dangerous; deadly

prey (PRAY) — an animal that is hunted by another for food

species (SPEE sheez) — within a group of closely related animals, one certain kind, such as an *eastern diamondback* rattlesnake

venomous (VEN uh mus) — able to produce venom; poisonous

venom (VEN um) — a poison produced by certain animals, including several snakes, fish, and spiders

INDEX